Classics

Wise Publications
London/New York/Paris/Sydney

Exclusive Distributors:
Music Sales Limited
8/9 Frith Street, London W1V 5TZ, England.
Music Sales Pty Limited
120 Rothschild Avenue, Rosebery, NSW 2018, Australia.

This book © Copyright 1992 by
Wise Publications
Order No.AM89927
ISBN 0-7119-3088-0

Music engraved by Interactive Sciences Limited, Gloucester.
Cover designed by Hutton Staniford
Music arranged by Stephen Duro
Compiled by Peter Evans

Photographs courtesy of:
Pictorial Press

Music Sales' complete catalogue lists thousands of titles and is free from your local music shop,
or direct from Music Sales Limited. Please send a cheque/postal order for £1.50 for postage to:
Music Sales Limited, Newmarket Road, Bury St. Edmunds, Suffolk IP33 3YB.

Air from 'The Water Music'

Composed by George Frederic Handel (1685–1759)

With movement

Chanson De Matin

Composed by Edward Elgar (1857–1934)

Autumn from 'The Four Seasons'

Composed by Antonio Vivaldi (1675–1741)

Berceuse from 'Dolly Suite'

Composed by Gabriel Fauré (1845–1924)

Dance Of The Hours

Composed by Amilcare Ponchielli (1834–1886)

Minuet In G

Composed by Johann Sebastian Bach (1685–1750)

Für Elise

Composed by Ludwig van Beethoven (1770–1827)

Song: "Longing for Spring"

By Mozart

Largo

Composed by George Frederic Handel (1685–1759)

Minuet

Composed by Luigi Boccherini (1743–1805)

Morning from 'Peer Gynt Suite'

Composed by Edvard Grieg (1843–1907)

Theme from 2nd Movement Symphony No 9 'From The New World'

Composed by Antonin Dvorak (1841–1904)

Ode To Joy

Composed by Ludwig van Beethoven (1770–1827)

O, For The Wings Of A Dove

Composed by Felix Mendelssohn (1809–1847)

On Wings Of Song

Composed by Felix Mendelssohn (1809–1847)

Pavane

Composed by Gabriel Fauré (1845–1924)

Theme from 'Romeo and Juliet'

Composed by Peter Ilych Tchaikovsky (1840–1893)

The Swan from 'Carnival Of The Animals'

Composed by Camille Saint-Saëns (1835–1926)

Trumpet Tune

Composed by Henry Purcell (1658–1695)

The Blue Danube

Composed by Johann Strauss II (1825–1899)

Moderately

41

42

Theme from 'Variations On A Theme By Haydn' (St Anthony Chorale)

Composed by Johannes Brahms (1833–1897)

Trumpet Voluntary

Composed by Jeremiah Clarke (1673–1707)

4/98 (30696)

I CAN PLAY THAT!

Classics

A selection of twenty-two classical themes arranged for
easy-play piano, complete with chord symbols.
Arranged by Stephen Duro.

Air from 'The Water Music'
Autumn from 'The Four Seasons'
Berceuse from 'Dolly Suite'
Chanson De Matin
Dance Of The Hours
Für Elise
Largo
Longing for Spring
Minuet
Minuet In G
Morning from 'Peer Gynt Suite'
O, For The Wings Of A Dove

Ode To Joy
On Wings Of Song
Pavane
The Blue Danube
The Swan from 'Carnival Of The Animals'
Theme from 'Romeo And Juliet'
Theme from 'Variations On A Theme By Haydn'
(St Anthony Chorale)
Theme from 2nd Movement Symphony No 9
'From The New World'
Trumpet Tune
Trumpet Voluntary

Other titles in the series include:
I Can Play That! Beatles
Order No. AM89912 ISBN 0-7119-3087-2
I Can Play That! Pops
Order No. AM89939 ISBN 0-7119-3089-9
I Can Play That! Ballads
Order No. AM89944 ISBN 0-7119-3090-2
I Can Play That! Children's Songs
Order No. AM89953 ISBN 0-7119-3091-0
I Can Play That! TV Themes
Order No. AM89968 ISBN 0-7119-3092-9

Wise Publications
Order No. AM89927

ISBN 0-7119-3088-0

9 780711 930889

WILLARD A. PALMER AND AMANDA VICK LETHCO

CREATING MUSIC
at the piano

Alfred